A POSTCARD FROM
BOURNVILLE

For David and Christina Butler, who are growing up in Bournville.

With kind permission of Cadbury Limited and thanks to Miss Patricia Dunbar for her help.

A POSTCARD FROM BOURNVILLE

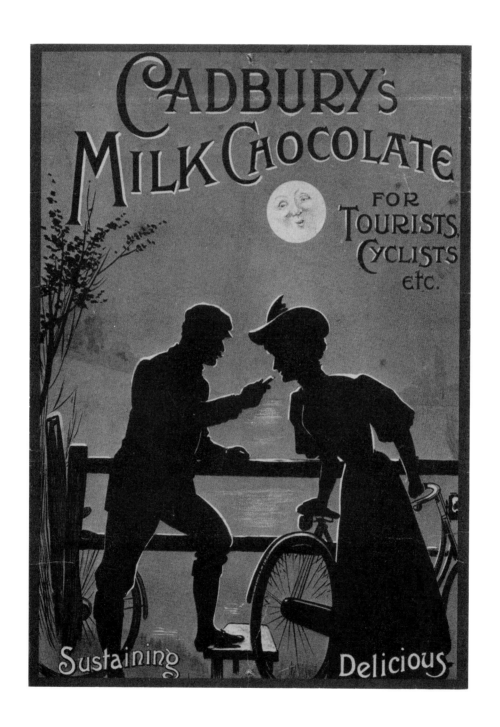

By

JOE AND FRANCES BRANNAN

First Published
by Brewin Books, Studley, Warwickshire, B80 7LG
in December 1992

ISBN 0 947731 84 9

British Library Cataloguing in Publication Data.
A Catalogue record for this book is available from the British Library

Typeset in Souvenir by Avon Dataset, Bidford on Avon, Warwickshire, B50 4JH
and made and printed by Warwick Printing Company Ltd, Warwick CV34 4DR

CONTENTS

INTRODUCTION

Introduction

It is not my intention to write the history of Bournville and the Cadbury factory, as it has all been recorded elsewhere by others more qualified than myself. This book is a pictorial record of the past and present of the Bournville area.

My interest in Bournville began as a child with a few picture postcards in my grandmother's collection. My mother had been on a school visit to the factory in 1929 and often talked about the beautiful garden village and how the chocolates were hand made.

As I grew up, one of my childhood amibitions was to visit the Cadbury factory to see the chocolates being made. Unfortunately, by the time I came to live in Birmingham in the 1970's, tours of the factory were no longer available. I was very disappointed!

However, I was delighted when "Cadbury World" opened. Now I too can glimpse scenes from the past and enjoy them.

I hope this book gives the same kind of pleasure to those who also enjoy "looking back", at ...

A Postcard from Bournville

Bust of the late Mr. George Cadbury, Bournville.

220-12.

CHAPTER ONE

Bournville Village

Bournville, now a suburb of Birmingham, lies about four miles south west of the city centre.

George Cadbury founded the Bournville Estate in 1895 having built the first cottages in 1879. In 1900 Mr Cadbury handed the 330 acre property, containing 300 houses, to a body of Trustees on behalf of the nation. He had very strong views and objectives and these statements are contained in the deeds.

"The Founder is desirous of alleviating the evils which arise from the insanitary and insufficient accommodation supplied to the large numbers of the working classes, and of securing to workers in factories some of the advantages of outdoor village life, with opportunities for the natural and healthful occupation of cultivating the soil."

"The object is declared to be the amelioration of the condition of the working-class and labouring population in and around Birmingham, and elsewhere in Great Britain by the provision of improved dwellings, with gardens and open spaces to be enjoyed therewith."

The early 330 acre site of the Bournville Estate occupied the land on either side of the Bourn Stream from which the village takes it's name.

Bournville, nr. Birmingham. The Model Village.

From the Trust Deeds —
''It is the desire of the founder that dwellings may occupy about one fourth part of the sites on which they are built. The remaining portions to be used as gardens or open spaces.''

BEECH ROAD, BOURNVILLE.

This is a road in Mr. Cadbury's model village of Bournville.

The houses built by the Trust were not just for people working at Cadbury Bros. In 1906 rents ranged from 4s 6d (23p) a week, rates not included, to 12s. (60p) a week. Some larger houses could be rented at a higher cost. I'm sure today's rent would astound the original tenants!

This scene was quite tranquil in comparison with the modern view.

The houses were planned to have variety in shape and size. Nowhere were there to be rows and rows of identical houses. Every house must have a garden. George Cadbury believed that gardening was a healthy activity and that it would help the family budget to have a well stocked fruit and vegetable garden.

Pairs of Cottages built in a variety of elevations cost £230.00 per cottage and £10.00 for the laying out of the gardens. What price nowadays?

By adding bays, dormers, porches etc. and using different materials, the houses could take on a completely different look thus achieving the variety required by the Trust.

Unlike many houses at the turn of the century, every Bournville house contained a bath. Some had bathrooms but some of the smaller cottages had a cupboard in the kitchen containing a tip-up bath, others had one sunk into the floor covered with a board, another variation was a bath standing at normal height with a cover to use as a table! Eventually all houses had proper bathrooms.

BOURNVILLE VILLAGE STEAM LAUNDRY, ACACIA ROAD, BOURNVILLE.
TELEPHONE: SELLY OAK 564.

Houses or cottages built for the Trust were mainly semi-detached or in blocks of three or four and were "planned so as to allow free circulation of air around them."

The village was planned and built to look picturesque. Wooded areas were kept where possible and new trees were planted.

"There are about seven houses to the gross acre. The majority of houses have 2 sitting rooms, a kitchen or scullery, 3 bedrooms and the usual conveniences."
'…. 2 quadrangles of small bungalows have been built for two single women, or for two friends living together."
Bournville Village Trust 1927.

The roads are planted with trees, and the houses are set back so that there is a space of 82 feet from house front to house front.

A view of Linden Cottage, Linden Road sent on Dec. 23rd 1908.

So glad to see the abundance of Cadbury advertisements in the shop windows! They were obviously deemed in keeping with the Trusts specifications.

June 17th 1922
''Dear Mother, I saw Father and Auntie off at the station. I bought a straw hat 2/6 and umbrella 7/11 in town. I went to the C.C. this evening...''
Was it a Carillon Concert I wonder?

Although the buildings remain the same the traffic makes the scene look very different.

Bournville Lane today is much busier with traffic going in and out of the factory.

In the early days of the Cadbury factory people walked or travelled to work by bicycle. There was very little traffic — horse-drawn vehicles being the only other road users.

The wooden bridge spanning Bournville Lane linked the Men's and Girl's Recreation Grounds.

Bournville Lane

Aug. 1st. 1913. The sender writes:-
"I hope you have had as good a time as I. I am in the land of Chocolate today, the half as never been told of the Cadbury's goodness. I shall have heaps to tell you when we meet."

BOURNVILLE LANE.

The Village Green is at the heart of old Bournville. It is a focal point with the Rest House in the middle and the Church, the schools and the shops around it.

In the planning of the Village, the Trust strictly controls the building of shops.

Shops may only be opened in areas set apart as shopping centres. There are also strict rules regarding posters and advertising signs. They must not "disfigure" the area.

This picturesque area today remains basically unchanged except by increased traffic and noise.

Bournville Parish Church is dedicated to St. Francis of Assisi. The buildings are in the Early Christian Basilican Style.

THE NAVE, BOURNVILLE CHURCH.

The Church and Hall were built by public subscription on a site given by the Trustees.

BOURNVILLE CHURCH

MEETING HOUSE, BOURNVILLE.   H.6610.

The Meeting House on the Village Green has a portrait bust of George Cadbury in an alcove in the wall. A closer view of this can be seen at the beginning of the book.

THE MEETING HOUSE, BOURNVILLE

55 BOURNVILLE MEETING HOUSE.

Like the Schools, the Meeting House was a gift to the Village. It was built to accommodate about 400 people and used for religious services.

The Rest House, opened in 1924, occupies the centre of the Village Green. It was erected by Cadbury employees on the occasion of Mr & Mrs George Cadbury's silver wedding.

The Rest House offers a peaceful place from which one can watch the world go by.

Richard Cadbury founded the Alms Houses in 1898. They were intended for old people of 60 years and upwards. Old employees of Cadbury Bros. were given preference. There were 33 houses each furnished and supplied with free coal, water and gas. The occupants also had medical attendance.

In 1919. The Alms Houses were visited by the King and Queen. The Queen went to number 22 to visit Mrs Tutin, aged 96, the oldest resident. Both the King and Queen "expressed their delight in their well ordered homes and in the comforts provided for those who were spending the evening of their life there so peacefully."

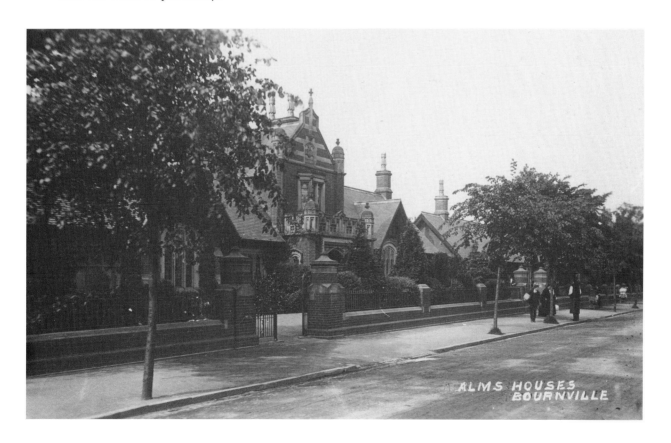

The schools were the gift to the Village from Mr & Mrs George Cadbury in 1905. They were built to accommodate 270 boys and 270 girls. Six classrooms for 50 children in each and six for 40 in each. The basement was for classes in cookery, laundry, manual instruction and handicraft. The tower was used for a library and laboratory. The view from the top was to be used to instruct the children in local geography, a map and compass were provided. The building contained carved and painted panels. Gardens were also provided for the children to learn gardening.

Dame Elizabeth Cadbury is pictured with her husband George and daughter Ursula at the laying of the foundation stone of the Infants School, 22nd January, 1910.

The sender of this card states:-
"These are the Elementary Schools of Bournville. Quite artistic, don't you think? There is a carillion of bells, up in the tower. An exact imitation of the one in Belgium."

Minworth Greaves.
This building once stood on the Kingsbury Road Between Curdworth and Minworth. It was bought in 1911 and re-built here between 1929 and 1932. Minworth Greaves House dates back from the 13th or 14th century.

In 1907 George Cadbury bought Selly Manor House. It originally stood nearer to Selly Oak, about a mile from here. It was dismantled and re-erected between 1912 and 1916. This house dates back to the early 14th century.

Old Farm Inn was formerly Bournbrook Farm, the home of Mrs Froggatt from 1831 to 1899. It is said that she had a ''deserved reputation as a herbalist''.

When the Trust was set up it was stated that open spaces were to be preserved in various parts of the Village. The parks were an essential part of the whole philosophy of the Cadbury ideal.

Aug. 12th 1912. The message reads:-
''There have been floods all over the place owing to heavy rainfall. Weather has been really bad here. According to last night's Mail A boy about 13 swept off his feet and drowned in the River Rea.''

E41 BOURNVILLE FIRCROFT.

CHAPTER TWO

Bournville Life

It was always part of the founder's objectives that Bournville should develop into a happy, healthy community. The surroundings would be pleasant and encourage people to spend their leisure time in the open air.

The amenities available in and around Bournville were many and varied.

Life in Bournville was certainly a revolutionary experiment which became a resounding success.

4790   THE POOL, ROWHEATH RECREATION GROUND—BOURNVILLE

During the years 1919 to 1924, great additions were made to the athletic equipment of the factory.
Rowheath Playing Fields were opened. The Works Model Yacht Club used the ornamental waters
and a shallower pool was provided for the children to sail their boats.

The Yachting Pool. 63.

Rowheath provided round the year sports facilities. There were 11 association football grounds, 3 rugby, 7 hockey, 11 cricket pitches, 3 bowling greens, 2 croquet lawns, 41 lawn tennis courts and a Gardening Club occupying 9 acres.

This is the Bournville Youth's Club second team. The year is not specified. In the early days, makeshift grounds were often used for playing cricket but eventually, a fully equipped sports ground was available. Both Richard and George Cadbury were keen cricketers. The famous English wicket-keeper, Arthur Lilley was a product of Bournville's cricket in the eighties.

Richard Cadbury was a keen footballer and used to join in the matches. It was encouraged along with other sports. In 1920 a Departmental Games League was started. More than 20 Football teams, representing various departments at the works, took part in competitions.

Music and Drama played an important role in the leisure activities at Bournville. As early as 1883 an orchestra of 6 players existed. The Musical Society was formed in 1900 with a band, an orchestra and a choir.

4789   PART OF THE GIRLS' GROUNDS, BOURNVILLE—THE FACTORY IN A GARDEN

Athletic recreations were organised separately for men and women. In 1896 the Men's and Girl's Recreation Grounds were opened adjoining the Works. The Bournville Girl's Athletic Club was formed in 1899 with a membership of 113.

RHYTHMIC DANCING BY EMPLOYEES BOURNVILLE WORKS

In 1908 members of the Girl's Athletic Club could take part in Morris Dancing two evenings a week. In 1923 a Folk Dance Society was formed. This was affiliated to the English Folk Dance Society in Birmingham.

IN GIRLS RECREATION GROUNDS BOURNVILLE

THE SPORTS GROUND , PAVILION & RECREATION BUILDING , BOURNVILLE

The Bournville Athletic Club was founded in 1896 with a membership of about 430 men. The Pavilion was the Firm's gift to commemorate the Coronation of King Edward V11.

These baths were erected in 1904. It was compulsory for all boys and girls to learn to swim when they came to the Works.

A POSTCARD FROM BOURNVILLE

The Day Continuation School was opened in 1925. There were 24 classrooms 19 for boys and 14 for girls. It was compulsory for under-eighteen year olds to attend classes.

WOODBROOKE.—THE LECTURE HALL.

In 1903 George Cadbury gave his house. Woodbrooke, for use as a centre of social and religious studies. It was the first of the Selly Oak Colleges.

The George Cadbury Hall was given by Dame Elizabeth Cadbury to the Selly Oak Colleges as a central assembly Hall.

Ruskin Hall was built in 1903 as an Art and Craft School and enlarged in 1928. It became the home of Bournville School of Arts and Crafts in 1911.

Kingsmead was opened for training men and women for foreign missionary work.

Fircroft was a college for working men founded in 1909. Students could take on a year's course in political and industrial history, economics and literature. It was as near as possible to University standard.

The Beeches was built by George Cadbury as a home for children from the congested areas of Birmingham. Groups of 30 children were brought there every fortnight throughout the summer. The children were weighed when they arrived and before they left and were found to gain an average of two and three quarter pounds during their stay.

In the winter the house was used as a place of rest for workers in churches of religious and philanthropic organisations.

In the clock tower of the school built in 1906 hung the famous Bournville Carillon of 22 bells.

BOURNVILLE.   FOUR OCTAVE CLAVIER.
TAYLORS, BELLFOUNDERS, LOUGHBOROUGH.

In 1923, 15 bells were added to the carillon by George Cadbury Junior to commemorate the death of his father. In 1934 it was decided to increase the number of bells to 48. But the tower was not originally intended to support such weight so it was reconstructed. An up-to-date action was put in and the clavier brought close up to the bells.

The carillon is one of the finest in Britain and its music has given great pleasure to many listeners.

BOURNVILLE
SOME OF THE BELLS OF THE CARILLON ADDED 1923
TAYLORS, FOUNDERS, LOUGHBOROUGH.

Mr Clifford Ball was appointed first carillonneur by the Trust in 1924. He gained a Diploma of the National School of Carillon Art, Malines, Belgium with honours. Before he retired in 1965 he gave many recitals both here and around the world. His playing was often broadcast on the radio and he had a very distinguished career.

May 21st. 1919 was definitely a day to remember at Bournville. King George V and Queen Mary came to visit and were greeted with enormous enthusiasm. The arrival of Their Majesties was accompanied by loud cheers and the Bournville band led the singing of the National Anthem.

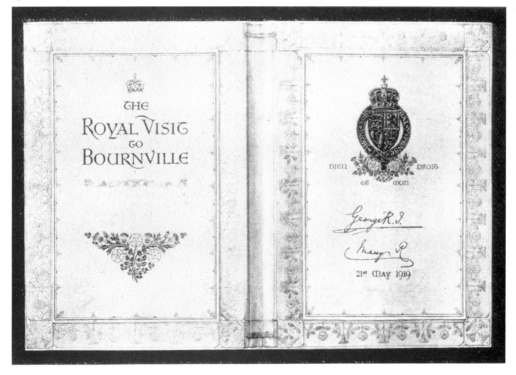

The King and Mrs George Cadbury and the Queen and Mr George Cadbury walked between lines of residents, chatting of what they saw.
Their Majesties were very interested in the provision of open spaces and good housing schemes.

The King decorates Company Sergeant Major A. Anderson, who was awarded the D.C.M., and Military Medal and Bar.

BOATS BRINGING FRESH MILK FOR CADBURY'S MILK CHOCOLATE.

There are 1½ glasses of fresh full cream milk in every ¼-lb. of Cadbury's Milk Chocolate.

4788

CHAPTER THREE

Bournville Works

In 1879 Richard and George Cadbury, sons of John Cadbury, who then owned the business, transferred their works from Bridge Street, Birmingham to the new site where it is today.

There were 230 employees.

It was originally intended that the factory should be called Bournbrook, taking the name from the nearby cottage and Hall, but before the factory was built, the name Bournville had been decided upon. This name owes its origin to the fact that Bournville sounded "French" and French chocolate was then considered the best!

The Cadbury ideal to develop a country environment for their workers became possible. The Works became renowned for being "A Factory in a Garden".

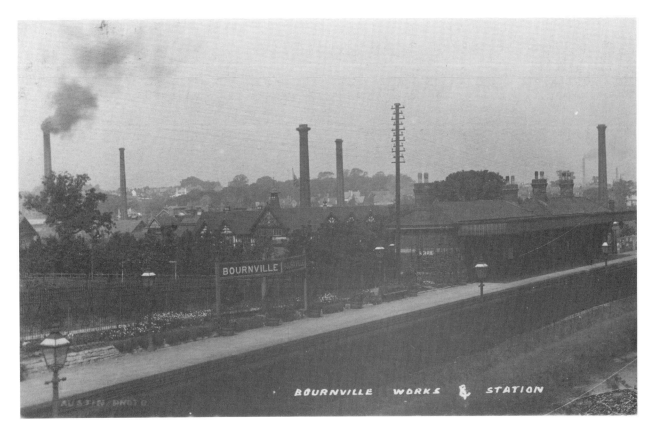

The Railway running through Bournville in 1879 was a single line branch of the Midland Railway, approaching Birmingham from the South West. It terminated half a mile from the town centre at Granville Street Station. The line was extended to the central station in the 1880's and converted into a double track.

Cadburys Works, from Railway, Bournville.

The site was chosen with its practical advantages for easy transport in mind. It had a railway station, then known as Stirchley Street, a canal and the site lay between two important roads.

This collection of steam and horse powered vehicles is Cadbury's fleet in the early 1900's. The first petrol motor-van was used in 1906.

Is modern transport any more efficient? The container on this lorry had just become dislodged!

BOURNVILLE WORKS.

The main rooms in the original factory were the Store Room, Packing Room, Girl's Warehouse, Moulding Rooms, Saw Mill, Grinding Room. Roasting Room and Essence Room. There was also a Boiling Room a Tinman's Shop, a Smithy, an Engine House, a Drying Room with boilers beneath, a Joiner's Shop, a Sugar Store, Stables, and various other departments including a Reading Room. The illustration above shows the factory after it had been enlarged.

BOURNVILLE. MESSRS CADBURY BROS LTD BOURNVILLE WORKS.

Inside the factory high standards were maintained. Immense quantities of card and wooden boxes, tins, bags and printed wrappers and labels were all produced on the site.

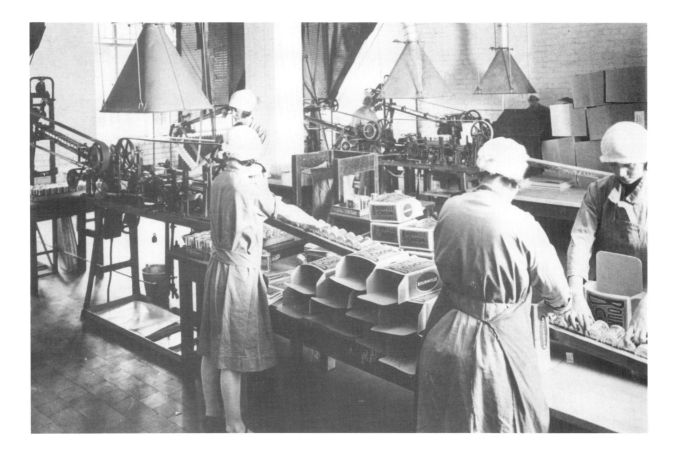

Margaret makes a Chocolate in four moves

A dab of chocolate—

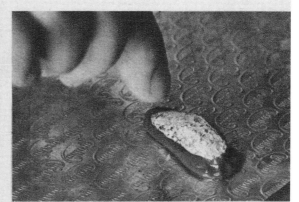

A Jordan almond on top—

More chocolate round the sides—

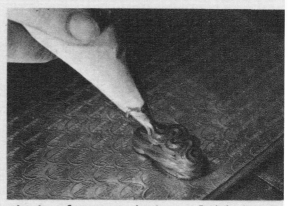

And a fancy squiggle to finish it off.

The art of making a chocolate from the ''Bournville Personalities'' book.

Cherries from the South of France were going into these chocolates.

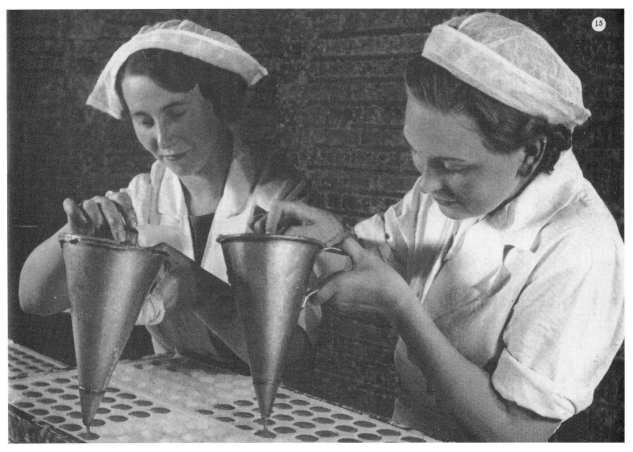

Cremes made with real fruits are being poured into flour moulds of different shapes.

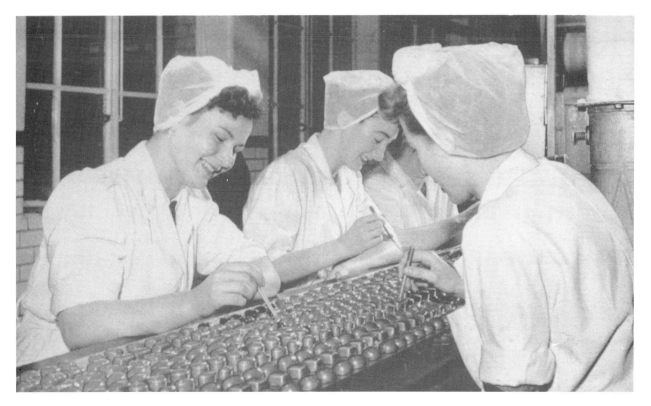

The special marks were all put on the chocolates individually.

This scene shows the weighing and packing of the chocolates.

THE DINING ROOMS AND COCOA FACTORY, BOURNVILLE

Cadbury workers have always had much attention paid to their daily needs. The Dining Room Block was completed in 1927. It contained club-rooms and the Concert Hall and was the ''centre of the social life of the factory.'' 5,000 people used the eleven dining rooms daily.

CADBURY'S TEA ROOMS   REDNAL

The clerks' Spring Outing to the Lickey Hills was a tradition which started in the 1880s with a casual ramble and became an annual event. The offices were closed for a half day and tea was taken at the Bilberry Hill Tea Rooms, a gift of Mr & Mrs Barrow Cadbury in 1904. The event was stopped during the first World War and resumed in 1920.

After 1920 boys & girls were only allowed to leave school at the end of term so three times a year, large numbers of young workers arrived at once. The Initiation Schools, lasting about a week, were held at these three periods to teach the young employees how to set about life in a factory.

A WALK IN GIRLS' GROUNDS, BOURNVILLE.

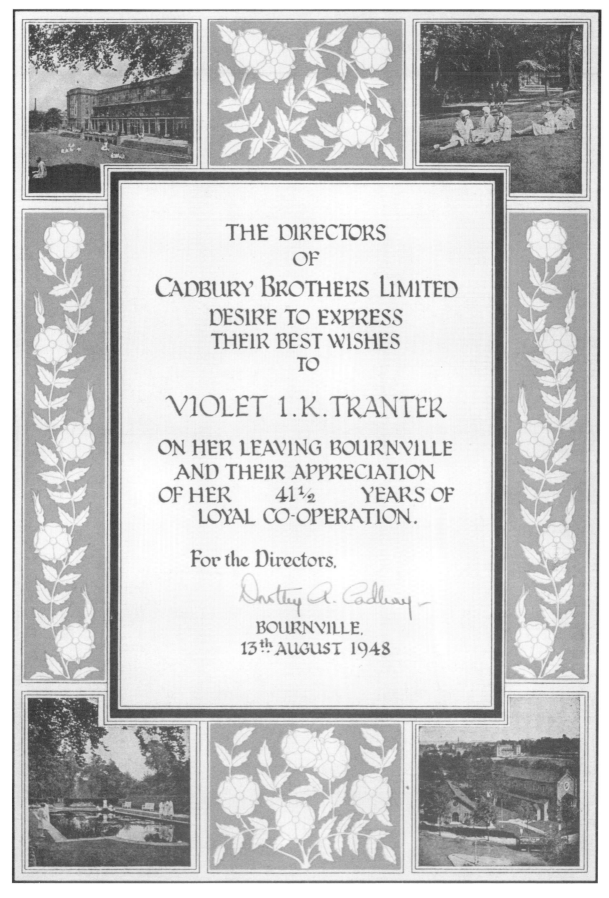

THE DIRECTORS
OF
CADBURY BROTHERS LIMITED
DESIRE TO EXPRESS
THEIR BEST WISHES
TO

VIOLET 1.K. TRANTER

ON HER LEAVING BOURNVILLE
AND THEIR APPRECIATION
OF HER   41½   YEARS OF
LOYAL CO-OPERATION.

For the Directors,

BOURNVILLE,
13ᵗʰ AUGUST 1948

I'm sure there are a great number of people who look back on their years at the Cadbury factory with great affection.

The suggestion scheme started in May 1902 as a result of a trip to America made by George Cadbury Junior the previous year, where he had seen a similar plan in operation. Payments were awarded every six months to the successful suggesters. The amounts varied between a shilling (5p) and on a few occasions £100.00.

LOADING THE AEROPLANE AT ROWHEATH.

Fresh Eggs! This De Haviland Moth aeroplane, belonging to the National Flying Services, was chartered to convey an urgent order of Easter Eggs to Messrs. S. Driver, Ltd. of Leeds on April 7th 1930.

During the night of Thursday 11th December 1919, a section of F block caught fire and the Works Fire Brigade arrived to tackle the blaze. They summoned help from Birmingham and the fire was contained to a relatively small area.

In 1940 Bournville Utilities Limited, a subsidiary of Cadbury Ltd., was formed. Work was carried out for the supply Department of the British Government using premises and resources on munitions production for the war.

The first job undertaken was the assembly of 5,117,039 Service Respirators and 6,335,454 Canisters. These were not used, as gas warfare never occurred.

Thousands of rockets were filled with cordite without any serious accidents.

Another dangerous job undertaken by Bournville Utilities was the covering of aeroplane petrol tanks to prevent leakage when damaged under enemy fire. Over 10,000 oil and petrol tanks were dealt with in the first twelve months.

In 1942 Bournville Utilities undertook the making of Jerricans but the Ministry of Labour decreed that labour for assembly work in the Birmingham area could not be allowed. The work was undertaken by the Battersea Depot. A number of the chocolate packing conveyors were ripped out of the Bournville factory and used in the Battersea Depot.

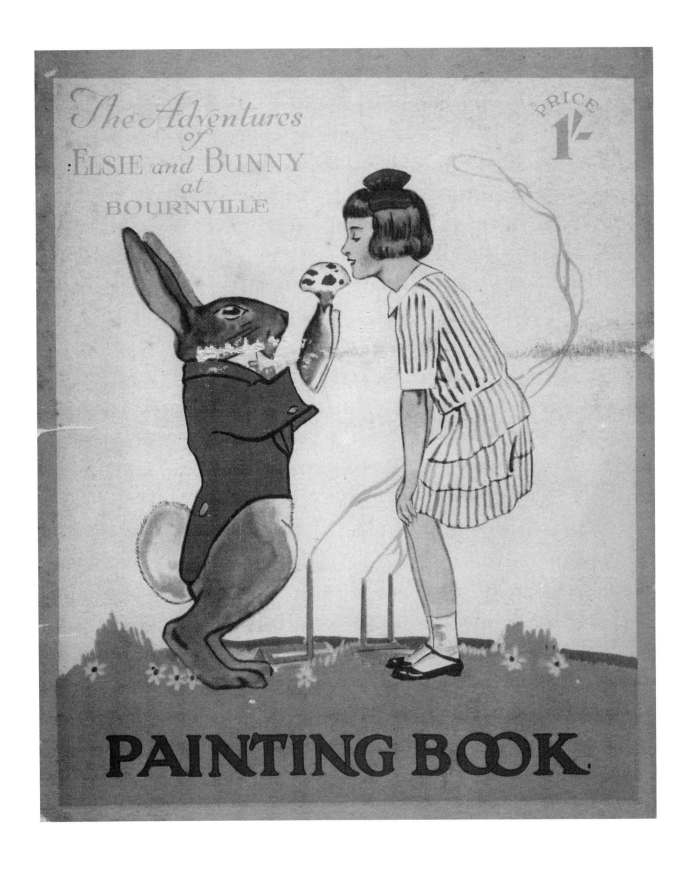

CHAPTER FOUR

Bournville World

Anyone who enjoys a nostalgic look at the past cannot fail to find something of interest in "The World of Cadbury". Throughout their history, Cadbury Ltd. have advertised their wares in a variety of ways. Nowadays the fancy boxes and tins, press advertisements, posters, give-away cards and shop signs are energetically sought after by collectors.

This chapter is devoted to the World of Cadbury in the true sense of its meaning.

It was Bournville Bunny.

The Painting Book, the front cover of which is illustrated on the previous page, contained eight coloured postcards and eight plain cards.

The Marzipan Room.

The story explains how everything is made at "The Factory in a Garden" and how Elsie helps to make chocolates. "First they went to the Marzipan room, where big windows showed up rows and rows of clean white tables and snowy-capped and aproned women and girls."

The Girls welcomed Elsie and Bunny gladly.

The pictures and story are of a girl who was granted a wish by the Bournville Bunny. Needless to say, her wish was "to be a Bournville Girl for a whole week!"

Elsie's fingers trembled with excitement.

"Here Elsie spent all the morning cutting out fascinating centres, then went along to another room where these were dressed in their delicious Cadbury coats. This was more fun than anything."

10 Thousand Prizes

CADBURY'S

DAIRY CDM MILK

REG'D TRADE MARK

CHOCOLATE 1d

THIS LABEL IS DULY REGISTERED UNDER THE TRADE MARKS ACT

REGISTERED TRADE MARKS "CADBURY" AND "BOURNVILLE" CADBURY, BOURNVILLE ENG

FOR PICTURE MAKING

A simple competition in connection with

CADBURY'S 1d BARS

This competition leaflet was issued in 1934. It's difficult to imagine nowadays the amount of chocolate which could be bought for an old penny in the pre-war days!

With the Compliments of the Proprietors of *Cadbury's Cocoa.*

The set of 32 British Butterflies & Moths Reward cards were issued in 1910.

REWARD CARD.

Presented to *Hubert Gale*

The Apollo Butterfly.

THIS beautiful alpine butterfly lives in the mountain valleys of the Alps, the Pyrenees, the Carpathians, and the mountains of Scandinavia. It is a grand flier and is often seen in July and August when one is taking a holiday among the Swiss mountains. The female generally has more red spots than the male, and also has a peculiar horny case at the end of her body.

She lays her eggs loosely among the saxifrages, and the little caterpillars quickly form inside, but do not eat their way out until the spring, lying curled up in the egg all the winter and often buried for weeks under deep snow.

The caterpillar grows very quickly when it does leave the egg, and when it is full grown is intensely black with orange spots. On the back of the segment behind the head is a little slit, and out of this the caterpillar can thrust a little two-pronged finger that gives out a peculiar smell and is supposed to be offensive to its enemies.

When it is full fed it spins some leaves of its food-plant together, and so makes a cocoon on the surface of the ground, in which it changes to a pupa. This pupa or chrysalis is covered with a delicate purple bloom, really made of wax, which prevents the chrysalis getting injured by the wet.

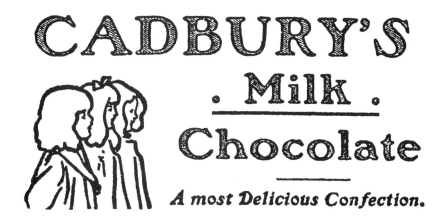

CADBURY'S
. Milk .
Chocolate

A most Delicious Confection.

BOURNVILLE
COCOA

"DELICIOUS AND NUTRITIOUS"

Prepared from the finest Cocoa
under Healthy conditions by British
workpeople in the Garden Village of
BOURNVILLE, WORCESTERSHIRE,
ENGLAND

SHIPPING SERIES

No
1. Viking Ship.

2. Spanish Galleon, 1588.

3. Old Wooden Sailing Ship.

4. Sailing Ship, East India
Clipper.

5. "Great Western"
(First Steamer to cross the
Atlantic 1838)

6. Atlantic Liner,
"Mauretania."

Cadbury's
CHOCOLATES

SPECIALLY MADE & PACKED
— FOR EXPORT. —

This set of six cards "Shipping Series" were issued in 1910. They were in four sizes presumably to be given away in different sized packages.

This novelty card takes the form of a puzzle — how do you detach the cup and saucer? It has me completely beaten!

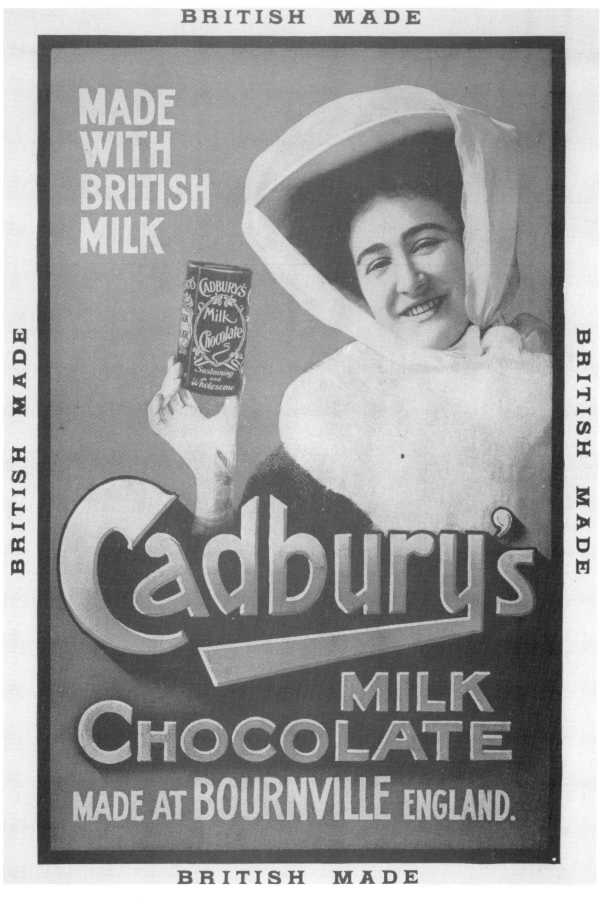

British and proud of it!

Pavilion,
Men's Recreation Ground.

Girls' Baths.

Britain's Model Factory.

Glimpses of "THE FACTORY IN A GARDEN."

Cadbury's MILK CHOCOLATE

A delicious confection, made of British full-cream milk and finest Chocolate.

Cadbury's COCOA

Is Absolutely Pure, most Delicious, Wholesome, and Economical in use.

"BOURNVILLE" CHOCOLATE BISCUITS

"The Last Word in Biscuits."—Made by CADBURY'S, superior in flavour and quality to anything yet produced.

Bournville,

where Cadbury's Cocoa, Milk Chocolate, Bournville Chocolate Biscuits, etc., are made, can justly claim to be Britain's Model Factory. The well-lighted, lofty and airy work-rooms are situated in the midst of park-like surroundings, trees, flowers and shrubs are everywhere. That these are the ideal conditions under which to work is evidenced by a death-rate of 1·5 per 1,000 among the 5,000 workers, probably the lowest death-rate in any factory in the world. Never has there been such an enthusiastic band of healthy, happy and contented workers, whose one purpose is to excel in their various tasks, and so help to maintain the excellence of all the productions bearing the name **Cadbury.**

Remember that the high quality of all CADBURY'S manufactures is and always will be fully maintained.

The reverse side of this patriotic advertisement is full of interesting information.

Italian Lake,
Girls' Grounds.

Girls' Entrance
to Works.

Copy of a Cadbury poster circa 1894. Cadbury's provided Cocoa and chocolate for Dr. Nansen's Polar Expedition.

This picture reminds me of the grocery shop my grandfather kept when I was a small child. There were large tins of loose biscuits with glass covers on top. I usually came out with a bag of broken pieces. Chocolate biscuits were my favourite kind!

AD. XV

PUNCH, OR THE LONDON CHARIVARI.—DECEMBER 24, 1898.

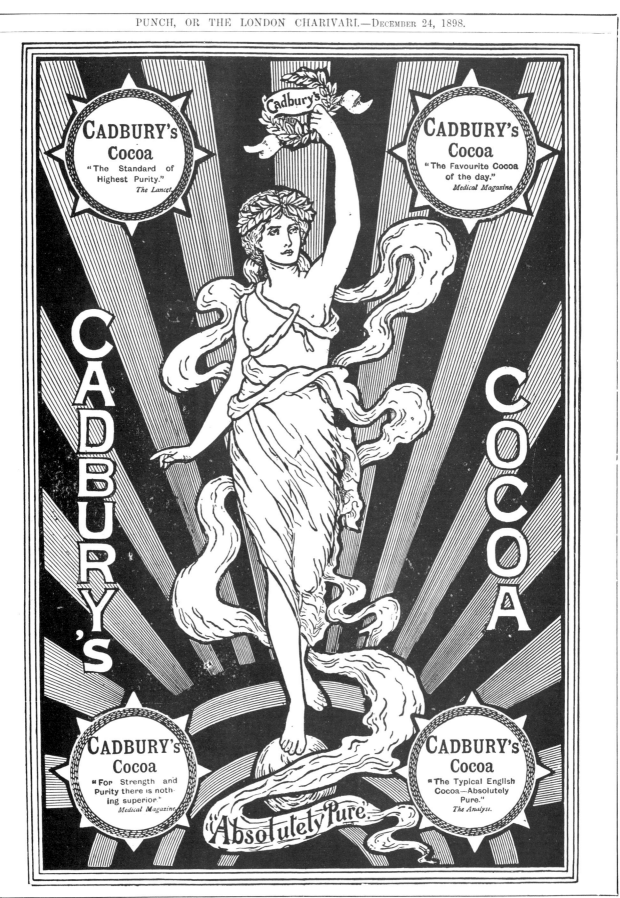

Printed by William Stuart Smith, of No. 30, Loraine Road, Holloway, in the Parish of St. Mary, Islington, in the County of Middlesex, at the Printing Offices of Messrs. Bradbury, Agnew, & Co., Limited, Lombard Street, in the Precinct of Whitefriars, in the City of London, and published by him at No. 85, Fleet Street, in the Parish of St. Bride, City of London.—SATURDAY, December 24, 1898.

PUNCH, OR THE LONDON CHARIVARI.—FEBRUARY 20, 1886.

ILLUSTRIOUS TRAVELLERS.—A pure, refined beverage, for all seasons and all occasions, is **Cadbury's Cocoa, a most delicious and nutritious article of diet. Warming, Comforting, Sustaining, Exhilarating. Rich in nitrogenous, flesh-forming constituents, strength, and staying power. A universal favourite, from the Cottage to the Palace.**

Printed by William Stuart Smith, of No. 30, Loraine Road, Holloway, in the Parish of St. Mary, Islington, in the County of Middlesex, at the Printing Offices of Messrs. Bradbury, Agnew, & Co., Lombard Street, in the Precinct of Whitefriars, in the City of London, and published by him at No. 85, Fleet Street, in the Parish of St. Bride, City of London.—SATURDAY, February 20, 1886.

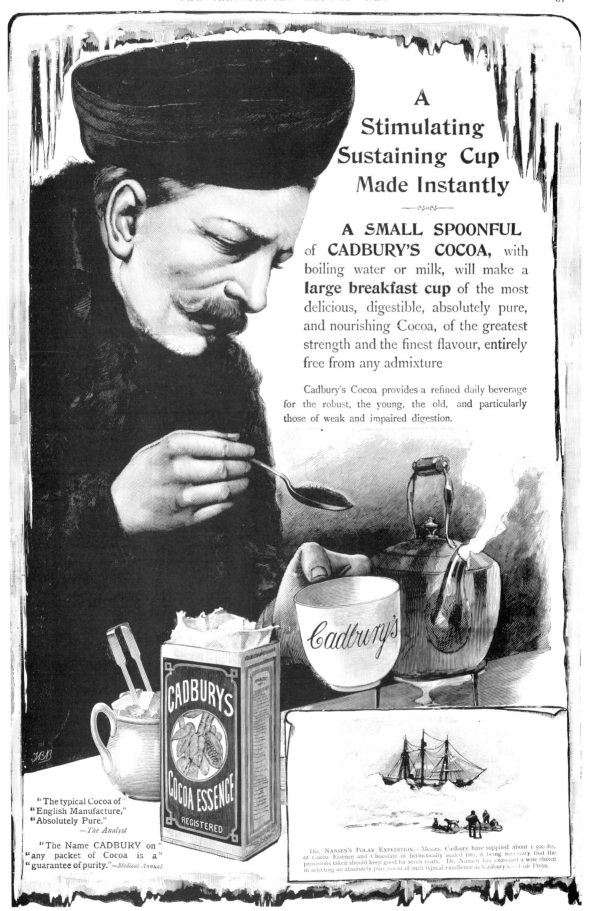

A Stimulating Sustaining Cup Made Instantly

A SMALL SPOONFUL of **CADBURY'S COCOA**, with boiling water or milk, will make a **large breakfast cup** of the most delicious, digestible, absolutely pure, and nourishing Cocoa, of the greatest strength and the finest flavour, **entirely** free from any admixture

Cadbury's Cocoa provides a refined daily beverage for the robust, the young, the old, and particularly those of weak and impaired digestion.

"The typical Cocoa of "English Manufacture," "Absolutely Pure." —*The Analyst*

"The Name CADBURY on" "any packet of Cocoa is a" "guarantee of purity."—*Medical Annual.*

CADBURYS COCOA ESSENCE REGISTERED

Dr. NANSEN'S POLAR EXPEDITION.—Messrs. Cadbury have supplied about 1,500 lbs. of Cocoa Essence and Chocolate in hermetically sealed tins, it being necessary that the provisions taken should keep good for seven years. Dr. Nansen has exercised a wise choice in selecting an absolutely pure cocoa of such typical excellence as Cadbury's.—*Tide* Press.

Further Reading

The Firm of Cadbury 1831 – 1931
Iolo. A. Williams.
Constable & Co Ltd 1931

Life of George Cadbury.
A. G. Gardiner
Cassell & Co Ltd. 1923

The Model Village & its Cottages:
Bournville.
W. Alexander Harvey.
B. T. Batsford 1906

Publications Dept., Bournville Works
The Bournville Carillon.
Bournville Utilities: A War record.
Bournville Works Magazines.
Elizabeth Mary Cadbury 1858 – 1951.
George Cadbury 1839 – 1922.
A Century of Progress 1831 – 1931.
Cadbury at Bournville 1879 – 1979.
Bournville Site Employee Handbook.
Bournville Works Women's Departments.
Food Factory.
Bournville.
Royal Visits 1919 – 1929 – 1939.

Bournville Village Trust Publications
Selly Manor Bournville.
Bournville Estate Residents Handbooks.
Bournville Village Trust.
Sixty Years of Planning. The Bournville Experiment.

Bournville. The Factory in a Garden.
The Bournville Story.
Bournville Personalities.
The Factory in a Garden.